divano
sofa
auto
car
GW01312250
sole
sun
cappello
hat
MY FIRST
ITALIAN
BOOK
LEARN ITALIAN
PICTURE DICTIONARY
FOR KIDS
muffin
muffin
leone
lion
cane
dog
mela
apple
zaino
backpack
barca
boat
sorella
sister
cinque
five

Dear Reader,

Congratulations, your adventure with a new language has just begun. To make it an unforgettable experience, I have prepared for you a book full of drawings that I hope you will not forget.

Language skills are the gateway to a world of amazing friendships, visiting wonderful places and accumulating memories - I wish you gather as many of them as possible.

Have fun!

Patrick G.

INDICE DEI CONTENUTI / TABLE OF CONTENTS

Locali / Rooms 5
Parti del corpo / Body parts 6
Vestiti / Clothes 8
Famiglia / Family 10
Conversazione / Conversation 12
Saluti / Greetings 14
Natura / Nature 15
Stagioni / Seasons 16
Giorni della settimana / Days of the week.......... 17
Verbi / Verbs 18
Materiale scolastico / School supplies 20
Materie scolastiche / Subjects 22
Numeri / Numbers 24
Colori e forme / Colors and shapes 26
Cibo / Food 28
Verdure / Vegetables.......... 30
Frutta / Friuts 32
Dolci / Sweets 34
Animali / Animals 36
Veicoli / Vehicles 38
Mobili / Furnitures.......... 40
Posti / Places.......... 42

bagno
bathroom

camera da letto
bedroom

salone
livingroom

cucina
kitchen

parti del corpo

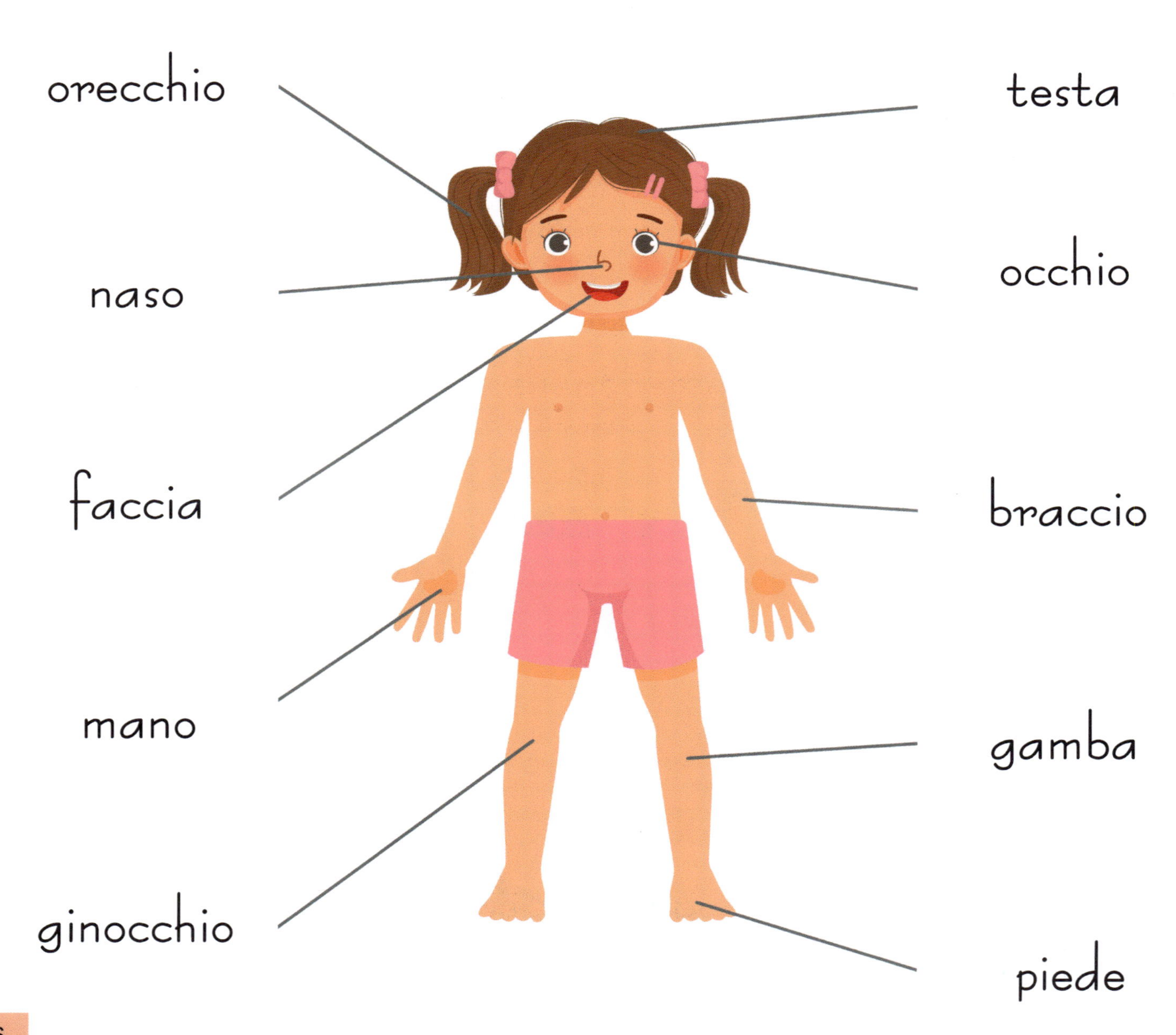

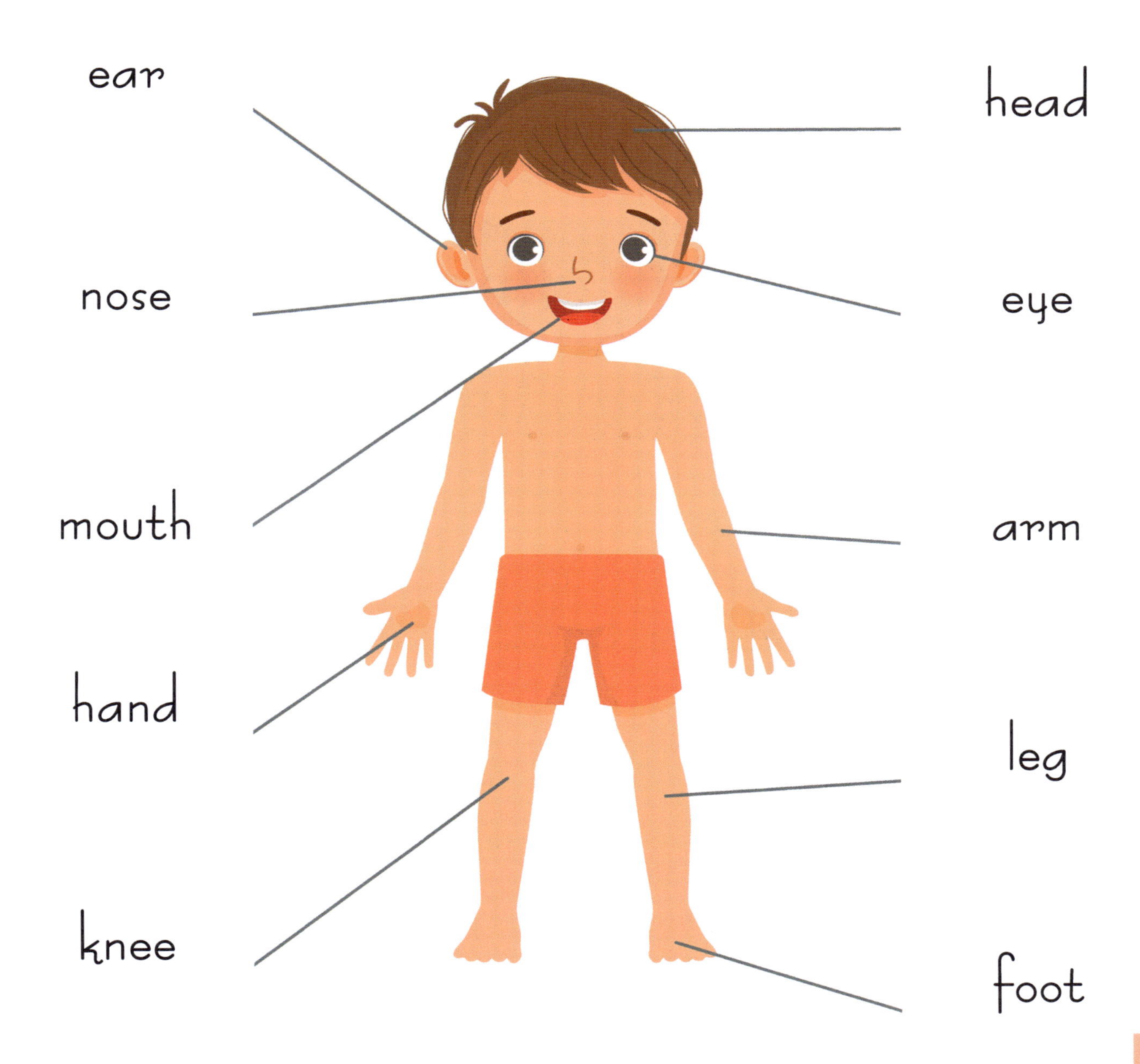
ear
head
nose
eye
mouth
arm
hand
leg
knee
foot

maglietta
t-shirt

felpa
sweatshirt

cappotto
coat

pantaloncini
shorts

vestito
dress

gonna
skirt

sandali
sandals

calze
socks

archetto
hairband

camicia

shirt

pantaloni

pants

salopette

dungarees

giacca

jacket

gilet

vest

scarpe

shoes

cappello

hat

papillon

bow tie

bretelle

suspenders

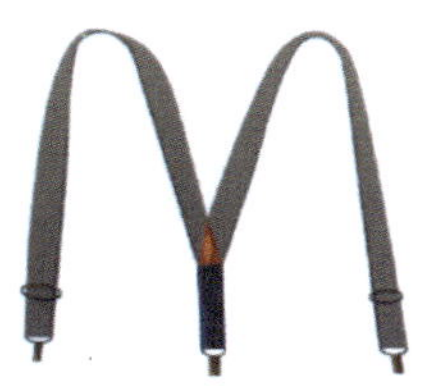

Famiglia

papà
zio
mamma
nonno
zia
nonni
nonna
cugino
figlio
fratello
figlia
sorella

grandparents
aunt
uncle
father
mother
grandpa
grandma
cousins
son
brother
daughter
sister

Riverenza!
Good morning!

Qual è il tuo nome?
What's your name?

Quanti anni hai?
How old are you?

Da dove vieni?
Where are you from?

Piacere di conoscerti!
Nice to meet you!

Il mio nome è Adam.
My name is Adam.

Ho otto anni.
I am 8 years old.

Vengo da Roma.
I am from Rome.

Buongiorno.
Good morning.

Buona giornata.
Good day.

Buona serata.
Good afternoon.

Buona notte.
Good night.

Per favore.
Please.

Grazie.
Thank you.

Scusate.
Sorry.

Arrivederci.
Goodbye.

Natura — Nature

sole

sun

cloud

pioggia

rain

albero

tree

foresta

forest

snow

fiori

flowers

erba

grass

lago

lake

primavera

spring

estate

summer

autunno

autumn

inverno

winter

giorni della settimana

Days of the week

Lunedì	Monday
Martedì	Tuesday
Mercoledì	Wednesday
Giovedì	Thursday
Venerdì	Friday
Sabato	Saturday
Domenica	Sunday

stare
stand

andare
go

sedersi
sit

bere
drnk

mangiare
eat

dormire
sleep

doccia
take a shower

leggere
read

scrivere
write

ridere
laugh

ballare
dance

saltare
jump

cucinare
cook

tagliare
cut

dare
give

nuotare
swimm

andare in bicicletta
cycle

giocare a calcio
play football

Materiale scolastico

pastelli

crayons

marcatore

marker

forbici

scissors

squadra

setsquare

righello

ruler

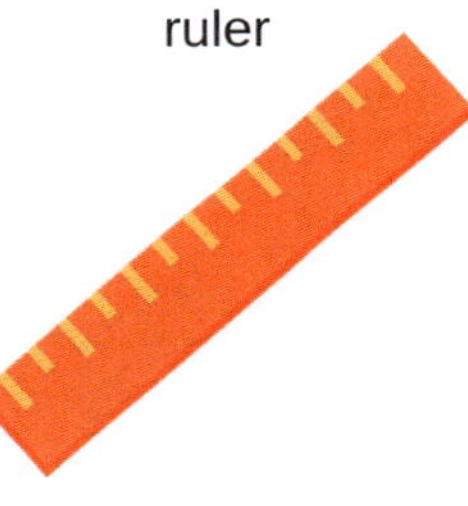

goniometro

protractor

cucitrice

stapler

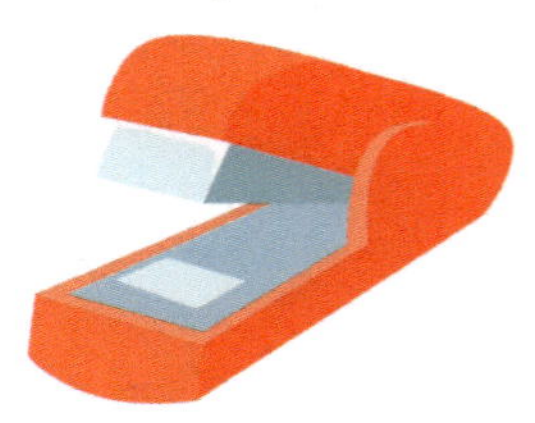

graffetta

paperclip

nastro adesivo

adhesive tape

zaino

backpack

gomma da cancellare

eraser

penna

pen

libro

book

taccuino

notebook

temperino

pencil sharpener

palla

ball

calcolatrice

calculator

globo

globe

Materie scolastiche

lingua straniera

foreign language

chimica

chemistry

bilogia

biology

matematica

mathematics

fisica

physics

informatica

computer science

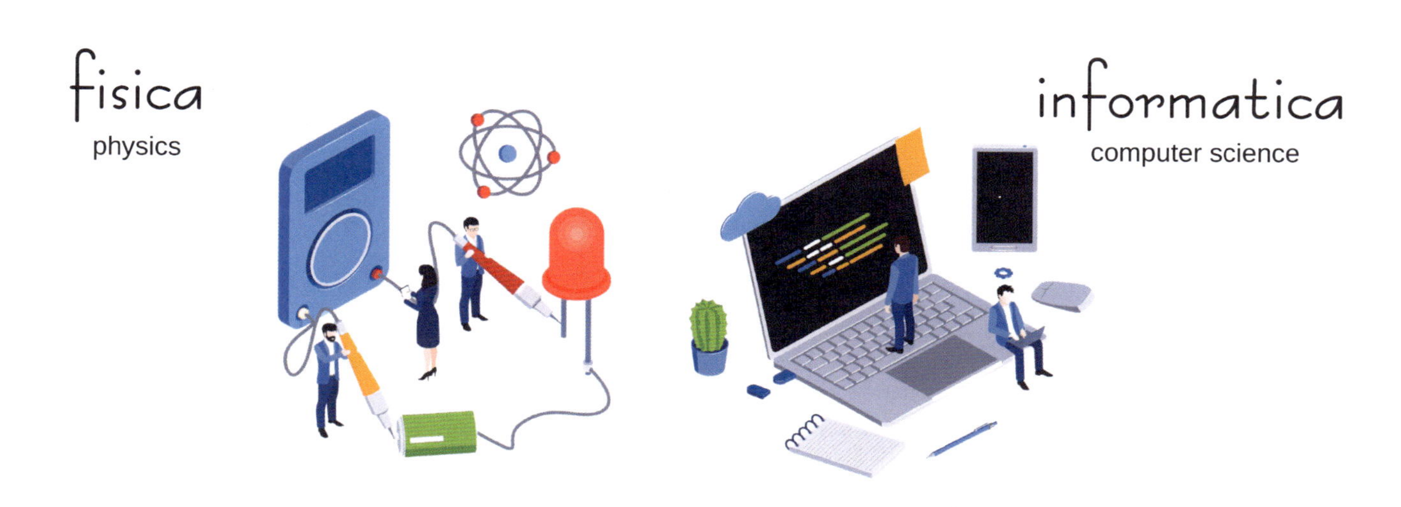

letteratura

literature

storia

history

Numeri

tre
three

quattro
four

cinque
five

sei
six

sette
seven

otto
eight

nove
nine

dieci
ten

10 20

venti
twenty

trenta
thirty

quaranta
forty

cinquanta
fifty

100

cento
one hundred

Colori

Colors

Forme

Shapes

square

rettangolo

rectangle

triangolo

triangle

cerchio

circle

ellipse

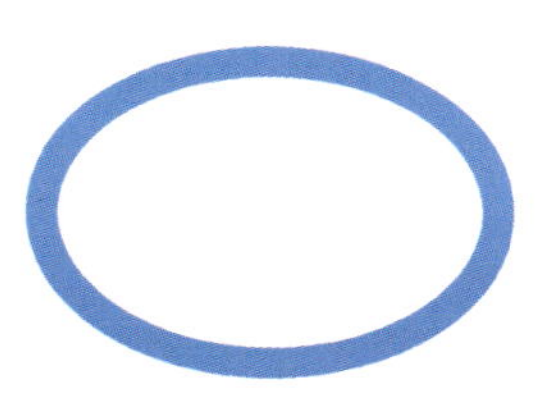

ottagono

octagon

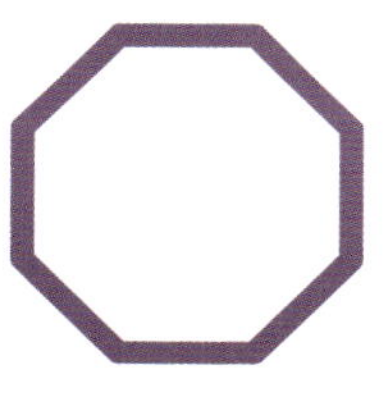

trapezio

trapezoid

parallelogramma

parallelogram

pentagono

pentagon

Cibo

latte

milk

succo

juice

burro

butter

uova

eggs

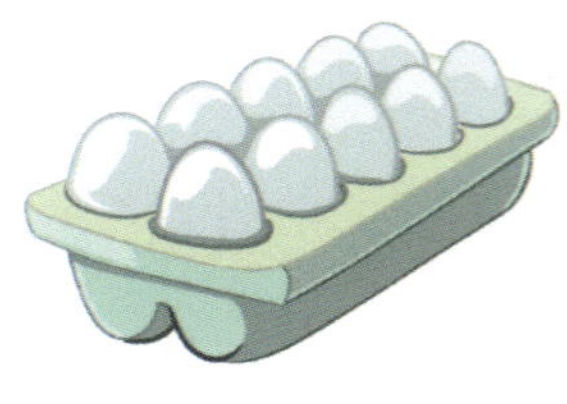

yogurt

yogurt

formaggio

cheese

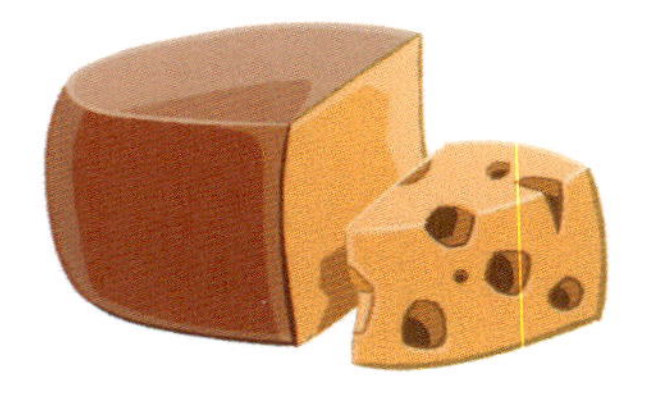

pesce

fisch

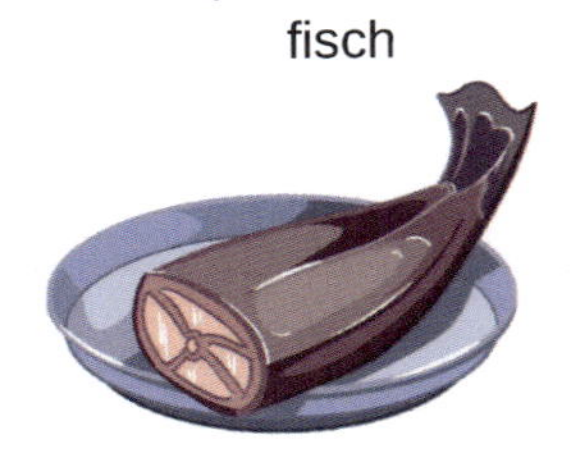

prosciutto

ham

pane

bread

caffè

coffee

tè

tea

sandwich

sandwich

zuppa

soup

piatto principale

main course

dessert

dessert

patatine fritte

fries

hamburger

hamburger

pizza

pizza

Verdure

carota
carrot

lattuga
cabbage

patata
potatoes

prezzemolo
parsley

pomodoro
tomato

cipolla
onion

cetriolo
cucumber

broccoli
broccoli

paprika
bell pepper

Vegetables

avocado
avocado

piselli
peas

zucca
pumpkin

barbabietola
beet

ravanello
radish

melanzana
aubergine

aglio
garlic

funghi
mushroom

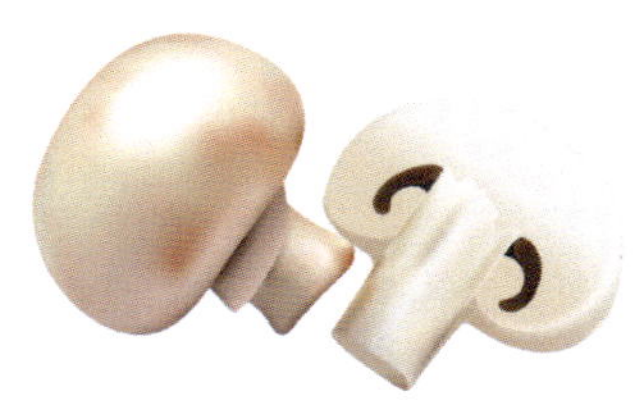

cavolfiore
cauliflower

anguria
watermelon

lampone
raspberry

fragola
strawberry

prugna
plum

uva
grape

fico
fig

melograno
pomegranate

ciliegia
cherry

pompelmo
grapefruit

ananas

pineapple

mela

apple

kiwi

kiwifruit

arancione

orange

mango

mango

limone

lemon

banana

banana

pera

pear

pesca

peach

muffin
muffin

ciambella
donut

torta
cake

cialde
waffles

cornetto
crossaint

pasticcino
cookie

pralina
praline

gelato
ice cream

cioccolato
chocolate

caramelle

candys

lecca-lecca

lollipop

zucchero filato

cotton candy

cocco

coconut

mandorla

almond

uva sultanina

raisin

nocciola

hazelnut

pistacchio

pistachio

arachide

nut

Animali

cane

dog

gatto

cat

lepre

hare

oca

goose

gallina

hen

pappagallo

parrot

tigre

tiger

cavallo

horse

coccinella

ladybug

elefante
elephant

leone
lion

giraffa
giraffe

ippopotamo
hippo

scimmia
monkey

serpente
snake

tartaruga
turtle

scoiattolo
squirrel

coccodrillo
crocodile

Veicoli

treno

train

autobus

bus

palloncino

balloon

elicottero

helicopter

aereo

plain

auto

car

camion

truck

taxi

taxi

metro

subway

razzo

rocket

bicicletta

bike

scooter

scooter

escavatore

excavator

camion della spazzatura

garbage truck

sottomarino

submarine

barca

boat

Mobili

poltrona

armchair

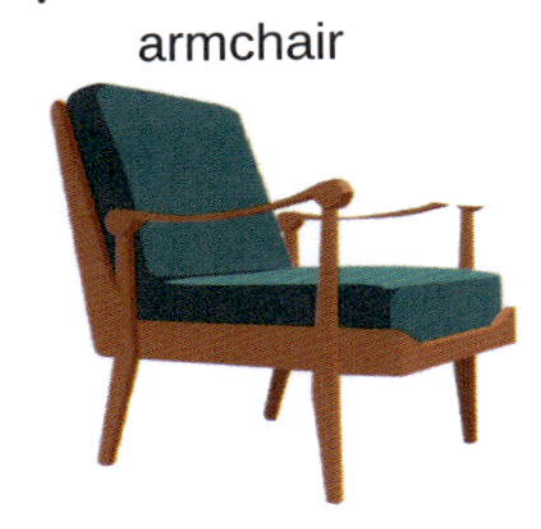

divano

sofa

lampada

lamp

tavolo

table

cassettiera

dresser

specchio

mirror

TV

TV

libreria

bookshelf

bollitore

kettle

tagliere

cutting board

pentola

pot

piastra

plate

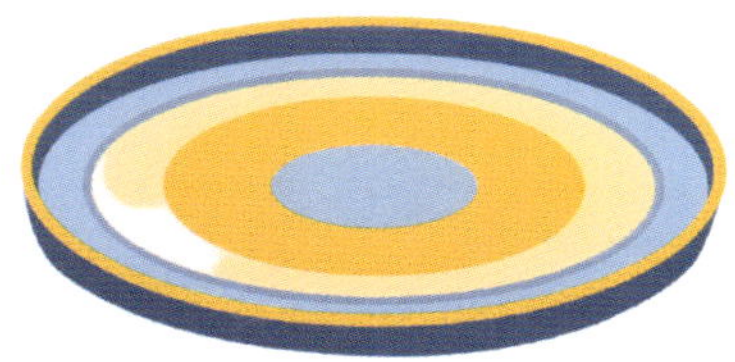

ciotola

bowl

tazza

cup

coltello

knife

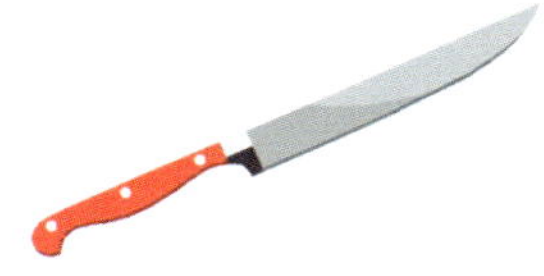

forcella

fork

cucchiaio

spoon

Posti

pizzeria

pizzeria

fiorista

florist's

parrucchiere

hairdresser

farmacia

pharmacy

calzolaio

shoemaker

negozio di giocattoli

toy store

libreria

bookstore

panetteria

bakery

caffè

cafe

ufficio postale
post office

fermata dell'autobus
bus stop

scuola
school

ospedale
hospital

banca
bank

stazione di polizia
police department

hotel
hotel

servizio antincendio
fire department

Printed in Great Britain
by Amazon